Babes
in the wool

Dedication

To my Mum, Win, who taught
me how to knit; to my daughter,
Beattie, for her critical eye; and to
my granddaughter Isabelle, with
all my love.

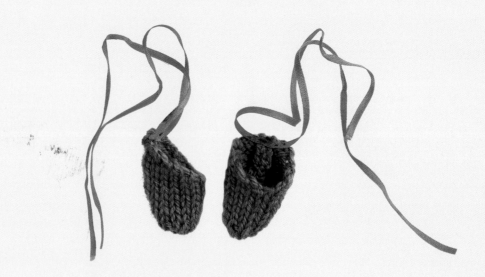

Babes in the Wool

How to Knit Beautiful Fashion Dolls, Clothes & Accessories

Fiona McDonald

Search Press

First published in Great Britain 2010

Search Press Limited
Wellwood, North Farm Road,
Tunbridge Wells, Kent TN2 3DR

Reprinted 2011

Text copyright © Fiona McDonald 2010

Photographs by Roddy Paine Photographic Studio

Photographs and design copyright © Search Press Ltd. 2010

ISBN: 978-1-84448-509-3

The Publishers and author can accept no responsibility for any
consequences arising from the information, advice or instructions
given in this publication.

Suppliers
If you have difficulty in obtaining any of the materials and equipment
mentioned in this book, then please visit the Search Press website for
details of suppliers: www.searchpress.com

Printed in Malaysia.

*The front cover image shows Miranda (page 62) and Rose (page 68).
On page 1 is Samantha (page 46) and on page 3 is Willow (page 40).*

Acknowledgements

A big thank you to everyone who helped me get this,
my first book, into print: Isabel Atherton of Creative
Authors who saw lots of potential and acted on it;
Roz Dace who gave me my first publishing contract
and then several more; Katie Sparkes who has
slogged away at making it all coherent and beautiful;
and the background crew of stylists, photographers
and anyone else who has worked on this publication.
Also thanks to Patons, Australia, for their generous
yarn contribution and to Danielle of WOW wool
shop in my home town of Armidale who has been a
constant support. It has been a
wonderful experience.

Contents

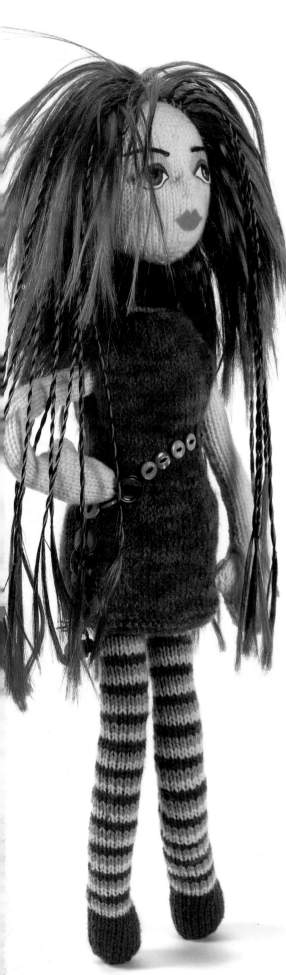

Introduction

It is universally acknowledged that there is nothing like a hand-knitted toy to bring comfort. Young children cuddle them; teenagers drape them across the bed; adults prop them in corners and surreptitiously talk to them when no-one is looking. It is also universally acknowledged that while receiving a knitted toy is wonderful, the act of making one is just as, or even more, enjoyable.

My mother taught me to knit when I was in primary school. I liked the idea of knitting much more than the reality. I would quite happily knit rows until I dropped a stitch, then I would have to wait for Mum to fix it. I decided I preferred sewing and left knitting to others.

Over the years I developed my skills as a cloth doll artist and found magic in transforming plain, flat cloth into a three-dimensional object. I gave the dolls armatures, made them life size and before long found I was doing sculpture.

Then a couple of years ago I found a pattern for a knitted bear. It was love at first sight and I set out to make the bear. I was surprised at how easy knitting really was. The problems I'd encountered as a child had disappeared as I began to understand the mechanics of it all. I knitted my bear and was extremely satisfied with him. However, having grown up to be an artist and a doll maker, I of course had to sit down and design my own knitted doll. My grown-up daughter emphatically stated that it was not to look like the kind of doll one knitted for fêtes or charity shops: it had to be sophisticated!

At the same time as I was bitten by the knitting bug, I discovered the world of Asian ball-jointed dolls (ABJDs) and fell for their large eyes and delicate faces. I was also horrified to learn that people spent huge amounts of money on accessories and clothing for these exquisite creatures. These were very much dolls for grown-ups.

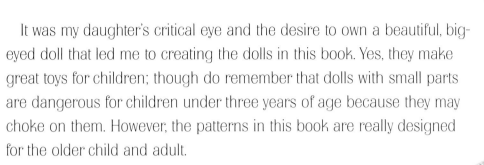

It was my daughter's critical eye and the desire to own a beautiful, big-eyed doll that led me to creating the dolls in this book. Yes, they make great toys for children; though do remember that dolls with small parts are dangerous for children under three years of age because they may choke on them. However, the patterns in this book are really designed for the older child and adult.

I offer three basic body designs, ranging in sophistication and difficulty (although none of the knitting techniques are challenging). There are three dolls to make with each body type, nine dolls in total, each with her own clothes, accessories, skin tone, hair style and templates for the glued-on painted felt eyes and lips. There are instructions for tinting the eye lids and cheeks with acrylic paint to give the dolls a more life-like appearance – something that is not normally done with knitted dolls.

A hand-made doll is an individual project and I encourage you to make them as individual as you can. Each doll has her own personality, and the fact that they are hand-knitted means that it is not easy to replicate them exactly. But therein lies their beauty. Take this as an opportunity to make your doll unique. Give her short, curly hair, or long, straight hair. Powder her nose with freckles, or give her pale, pale skin and dark red lips to make her into a Gothic vampire. Knit her in green, give her three eyes, and she becomes an alien from a far-away planet!

My most important rule is to let your imagination run wild and have fun. I hope that you will enjoy knitting and personalising these dolls as much as I have enjoyed designing them.

Before you begin

The dolls in this book are specifically designed for adults and older children. However, younger children will love the dolls too, but if you intend to give one to a child who is under three years old, then the following safety precautions should be taken.

- The doll must not have any small, detachable parts that may get chewed off and choked on.
- The felt eyes and lips must be stitched on as well as, or instead of, gluing. Otherwise embroider features straight on to the knitted face.
- Do not use buttons, press-studs, hooks and eyes, or anything else that could possibly be a choking hazard.

Materials

Each pattern includes a list of the necessary materials and equipment needed for that particular project. Please note that all the quantities of yarn given in this book are to be regarded as approximate.

Abbreviations

I have tried to keep the patterns as simple as possible, and the only abbreviations you need to remember are:

K knit

P purl

GS garter stitch (consecutive rows of knit stitch only)

SS stocking stitch (alternating rows of knit and purl)

inc increase (I always increase by knitting into the front then the back of the stitch before slipping it off the left-hand needle)

dec decrease (by knitting two stitches together unless specified otherwise)

cast off I usually knit or purl the row and cast it off as I go.

Yarns

Patons yarns kindly supplied the wool for the dolls in this book. I used Cleckheaton Country double-knitting wool because I found it lovely wool to work with and it has a great range of skin tones. While I would recommend using this yarn for making the dolls, any double-knitting yarn (also known as 8 ply or light worsted) will give equally good results. Whichever yarn you choose, it is a good idea to use the same brand throughout your knitting as not all yarns are the same. I prefer to use pure wool, but there is no reason why an acrylic or acrylic mix could not be used, as long as it is a smooth and not a textured yarn.

For the hair use whatever takes your fancy: straight wool, bouclé, fancy yarn, fluffy yarn or nylon doll hair, for example. Knitted and unravelled wool makes lovely, wavy hair. It can be thick, thin, short or long, red, green, brown or any other colour. Try adding ribbon, silk embroidery thread or chunky yarn that looks like dreadlocks.

For the clothing I have used Cleckheaton Country double-knitting wool plus some cheap, novelty yarns that I had in my huge hoard at home. I suggest you experiment with what you have available, and you may well come up with something even better than the original.

Tension

The yarns used in this book all give a similar tension range (gauge), which is 22 stitches to 10cm (4in) when used with 4mm (US 6) needles and stocking stitch. Any yarn that states this tension on the ball band is therefore suitable for use with the patterns in this book.

Knitting needles and crochet hooks

You will need three sizes of needle – 3mm, 4mm and 10mm – and a 3mm (US 1 or C/D) crochet hook. The basic dolls are knitted using a 3mm knitting needle, which is smaller than you would normally use with double knitting. This is because the knitted body of the dolls needs to be tighter than a knitted garment would be. If the tension is too loose, then the stuffing will be visible and the doll will be unshapely. If you find it too difficult to knit with the double-knitting yarn on 3mm needles, then experiment with slightly larger needles, say 3.25mm or 3.5mm (US 4), until you find a comfortable size.

I have knitted the dolls' underwear using 3mm needles so that they fit snugly; the other clothing I have knitted using 4mm needles. For some of the fancy-yarn knits, such as scarves and wraps, I have used a huge 10mm pair of knitting needles. These create a lacy effect and is quick to do!

I use a 3mm (US 1 or C/D) crochet hook for crocheting cords on clothes and also for hooking hair through the knitted scalp. You may prefer to use a 3.5mm or 4mm (US 00 or E/F) hook, especially when using thicker yarn for hair. Knitted versions of the crocheted cords and ties are also provided for those who prefer to knit.

Needle sizes

Metric:	3mm	4mm	10mm
UK (old):	no. 11	no. 8	no. 000
US:	3	6	15

Other items you will need

Polyester fibrefill

I use the type of stuffing found in cheap pillows, or carded fleece, to stuff the dolls with. Polyester fibrefill is probably the easier to obtain, and is the better of the two for stuffing the heads. Carded fleece gives a lovely weight to the dolls but is heavier and harder to needlesculpt. In the end it comes down to availability and personal preference.

Stuffing tool

I use an old, cheap, bristle paintbrush. The bristles help hold the stuffing as you push it down a long leg.

Tapestry needle

Used for sewing up seams and needlesculpting the face and body where necessary. I use an ordinary sized one, but you can use a doll-making needle if it is easier.

Glue

I use clear, fast-drying craft glue. You could use white craft or wood glue, but they take much longer to dry.

Felt

White felt is used for making the eyes; red or pink felt for lips; and brown or black for eyebrows (to match the doll's hair).

tip

When stuffing your doll, use smallish pieces so that you don't get big, misshapen lumps where you don't want them. Legs are quite difficult to stuff evenly and smoothly – massage the stuffing into place, and avoid over-stuffing. As a general rule, try not to put so much stuffing in that the knitting stretches apart.

Acrylic paint

You will need white, black, blue (ultramarine), alizarin crimson, raw sienna and raw umber (browns) for painting the eyes and tinting the face. I also use a paint medium to make it flow better, but you can use plain water too. Alternatively, use waterproof felt-tip pens or fabric markers. Test the pens on a piece of felt before you draw on the eyes in case the ink bleeds into the felt.

Varnish

A gloss acrylic varnish is used to coat the eyes once they are dry to seal them and give them a shiny finish. This, though, is optional and down to your own personal taste.

Tiny brushes

These are used for colouring the eyes. Acrylic brushes used for painting models or folk art are suitable.

Nylon hair extensions and scrunchies

I have used these for the hair on some of the dolls, for example Ann and Miranda.

Buttons, beads, hooks and eyes and press-studs

Buttons are used for the button belt on page 65; beads for decorating belts and cords; hooks and eyes and press-studs for fastening clothes.

Sewing needles, scissors and thread

These are used for sewing on buttons and other fastenings, hair, eyebrows, etc. You will need a pair of sharp scissors for trimming threads and for cutting out felt shapes for the eyes, lips and eyebrows. Alternatively, a scalpel or craft knife can be used.

Making faces and hair

Giving your doll a face and hair is where the fun really starts. Sometimes you have little control over the facial expression of your doll; she will have the type of face she wants no matter what you do. I have included some templates for eyes and lips to use if you are unsure about what kind of face you want, but I do encourage you to try designing your own.

Nose

The smaller dolls – Jenny, Poppy and Ann – have a simple nose in the form of a single stitch. The other dolls each have a needlesculpted nose, and the instructions for this are given in the relevant section of the book.

Eyes

The biggest problem I have found with knitted dolls is giving them realistic-looking eyes. I tried embroidering them on using yarn but could not obtain the detail I wanted, so I began using white felt instead. The woolly texture of felt makes it difficult to paint on, so I first cover the felt with one or two coats of white acrylic paint. I also use some needlesculpting to make the eyes sit on the face better. You might prefer to do this after you have attached the eyes.

1. Trace off the templates you want to use for your doll. These are provided on pages 78–79. For the smaller dolls, Jenny, Poppy and Ann, use the smaller eyes and mouths; the larger ones are for the more complicated dolls later in the book.

2. Trace around each template on to felt using acrylic paint, good-quality felt-tip pens or fabric markers. I prefer the subtlety of paint but it does require patience and a steady hand.

3. Paint the coloured iris and the black pupil. Outline the iris in a darker version of the iris colour, then paint in the upper lid in a skin or eye-shadow colour. This is followed by the darker line for the upper lashes. For the lower lashes use a soft brown, though you do not have to paint a lower lash line in at all.

4. To finish, place two white dots in each eye to reflect the light and make them look more real. The upper dot is a little bigger than the lower one. Set them just to one side of the pupil to make the eye appear curved.

5. When the paint is dry, cut out the eyes and pin them in place on either side of the nose until the doll looks right. Glue into place with an acrylic fast-drying craft glue or PVA.

6. When the eyes are dry you can coat them with a gloss varnish to give a shiny finish, though this is down to your own personal taste.

Eyebrows

The eyebrows can be traced on to felt using the templates on pages 78–79, or embroidered on in wool or embroidery thread. Cutting fine eyebrows can be difficult as sometimes the felt disintegrates. Cut them with a scalpel, craft knife or very sharp scissors and glue them in place.

Lips

The lips are also made of felt, cut in a heart shape and glued on. Various lip templates are provided in different shapes and sizes (see pages 78–79), or you can cut out your own. Either trace around the template on to the felt or fold a small square of felt in half to make a triangle and cut out a mouth shape as shown in the diagram on the right. You will need approximately 2cm (¾in) square for a small mouth and 2.5cm (1in) square for a larger one.

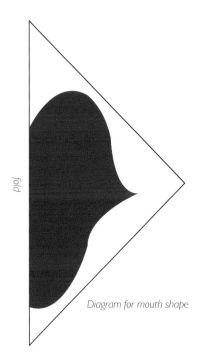

Diagram for mouth shape

Needlesculpting the face

This is not as hard as it sounds, and is best done once the eyes and other features are in place.

1. Take a thread of skin-tone yarn and thread it through a tapestry needle. Insert it into the middle of the head at the back, pass it through the head and bring it out at the inner corner of one eye.

2. Make a small stitch and pass the needle back out through the back of the head, close to where it went in initially. Pull gently on the thread until the eye area indents slightly (don't overdo it, or the face will be distorted).

3. Pass the thread through the head again, and bring the needle out at the inner corner of the other eye. Pass the needle through the back of the head again and pull the thread until the eye area indents.

4. Repeat this process for the outer corners of the eyes. When you are satisfied with the shape of the face, secure the thread by making a double stitch, inserting the needle through the head and snipping off the thread where it emerges.

Finishing touches

1. To give the dolls an extra lift, mix a little mauve acrylic paint with a lot of water to make a wash. Dampen the eye socket area where the eye and nose meet using clean water. This is the area of the face usually cast in shadow.

2. Drop a small amount of the mauve wash into the dampened area and let it bleed outwards. Blot off the excess with a clean tissue. A word of warning: do not let the eye itself get damp because the wash will bleed into it too.

3. To give a soft blush to the cheeks, mix a red acrylic paint with water to make a pink wash. Dampen the cheek area as before, drop the pink wash into it and blot off any excess. Try not to make the cheeks too red or the poor doll will look permanently embarrassed!

Hair

A doll's crowning glory! I like my dolls to have hair that looks as though it is growing out of their heads. There are two ways of doing this.

The rooted method

For this you will need a crochet hook. A 3mm (US 1 or C/D) crochet hook is just about right, depending on the thickness of the yarn. For very thick yarn, a 3.5–4mm (US size 00 or E/F) might be better. You can use any kind of yarn you think will make beautiful hair.

1. Find a book or a piece of stiff board that is the height of the length of hair you want. Wrap the yarn around the book or board, not too tightly. Before it gets too bulky, cut through the wound yarn at one end of the book only; the doubled lengths of yarn each form two strands of hair.

2. Begin by working round the hair line, starting above the middle of the forehead. Insert the crochet hook under a knitted stitch. Hook the folded hair strand and pull it back through the stitch. Now insert the hook into the loop formed and pull it tight to secure the hair. Continue around the head and then fill in the rest of the scalp.

3. When the hair is done, trim to the desired length or style.

Using fake hair

For some dolls I use cheap, synthetic hair extensions and hair scrunchies to create amazing hair colours and textures.

1. Carefully disassemble the hair accessory so that you are left with a strip of fake hair sewn along the top, and wind this around the scalp of the doll. Start at the centre of the doll's head and work outwards in a spiral.

2. Stitch it in place using a thread that matches the scalp colour of the doll.

3. Cut smaller lengths from the strip for a fringe or to fill odd spaces.

Let's jump!

Jenny, Poppy & Ann

Of all the dolls in this book, these are the simplest to make. Standing approximately 50cm (19¾in) high, they are based on the classic rag doll, whose back and front are identical. But that is where the similarity ends. Jenny, Poppy and Ann have big eyes, masses of hair and long, long legs that are perfect for displaying their low-waisted jeans, trendy boots and ballet slippers. All of the clothes are interchangeable and, of course, can be made in any colours you like.

Making the body

Make two.

If you are making a doll with a knitted-on swimsuit, begin with coloured yarn; otherwise begin with skin-coloured yarn.

Cast on 24 sts.
rows 1–10: SS for10 rows, beginning with a knit row and ending with a purl row.

materials

Needles: 3mm (US 3)
Crochet hook: 3mm (US 1 or C/D)
Yarns:
either 2 x 50g balls of skin-coloured yarn *or* 1 x 50g ball of skin-coloured yarn and 1 x 50g ball of coloured yarn for the knitted-on bathing costume and/or striped legs

yarn (or synthetic hairpiece) for hair

Other materials:

half a pillow, or approx. 250g (9oz), of polyester fibrefill (you will probably use less)

old paintbrush for stuffing

either 3 empty toilet rolls *or* a piece of thick cardboard measuring 20 x 6cm (7¾ x 2¼in)

adhesive tape

tapestry needle

white felt for eyes, and pink or red felt for mouth

acrylic paints in brown, blue, black and white for painting the eyes

gloss acrylic varnish for sealing the eyes and making them shine

glue suitable for sticking felt to wool, e.g. PVA or a clear craft glue

Hips

row 11: K2tog, K to last 2 sts, K2tog [22 sts].
row 12: purl.
rows 13–16: repeat rows 11 and 12 twice more, ending with a purl row [18 sts].

Waist

rows 17–20: SS for 4 rows, beginning with a knit row and ending with a purl row.

Chest

row 21: knit, inc 1 st at each end [20 sts].
row 22: purl.
rows 23–26: repeat rows 21 and 22 twice more, ending with a purl row [24 sts].
rows 27–32: SS for 6 rows, beginning with a knit row and ending with a purl row.

Shoulders

row 33: K2tog at each end [22 sts].
row 34: P2tog at each end [20 sts].
If you are knitting on the swimsuit, change to skin-coloured yarn.
rows 35–40: repeat rows 33 and 34 until 8 sts remain.

Neck

rows 41–48: SS for 8 rows.

Head

row 49: knit, inc 1 st at each end [10 sts].
row 50: purl, inc 1 st at each end [12 sts].
rows 51–54: repeat rows 49 and 50 until there are 20 sts on the needle.
rows 55–70: SS for 16 rows.
row 71: K2tog at each end [18 sts].
row 72: P2tog at each end [16 sts].
rows 73–75: repeat rows 71 and 72 until 10 sts remain.
Cast off purlwise.

Making up

1. Pin the two bodies together, with right sides facing. Back stitch around the shape, leaving the bottom end open for stuffing. Turn right-side out.

2. Stuff a small amount of polyester fibrefill into the head.

3. Make a backbone with either a length of rolled cardboard or three toilet-roll tubes telescoped into each other to the desired length (approx. 20cm; 7¾in). Fold the cardboard cylinder in three lengthways and press firmly (see the diagram below).

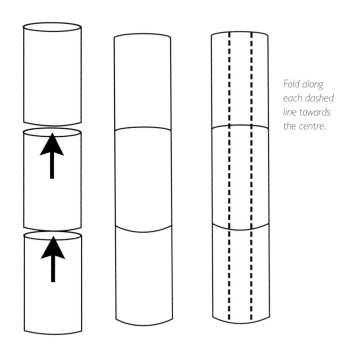

Fold along each dashed line towards the centre.

4. Use adhesive tape or masking tape to bind around the cardboard backbone and hold it in place. Turn the tape over so that the sticky side is facing outwards and wrap it round the backbone. The fibrefill will stick to it, which will help hold the backbone in place inside the doll.

5. Push the cardboard backbone into the body and halfway up into the head. Stuff around it with very small pieces of stuffing to shape the head.

6. Choose which side will be the front and push more stuffing into the chin area. Lightly stuff the neck (just enough to cover the backbone).

7. Continue stuffing around the backbone until the body is filled out but the stitches are not stretched. When the body is sufficiently stuffed, whip stitch it closed at the bottom.

8. Tidy up any threads by threading them through a needle and passing them back into the body. Cut off any left-over threads.

Arms

Make two.

Cast on 3 sts.
row 1: knit, inc in each st [6 sts].
row 2: purl.
row 3: knit, inc in each st [12 sts].
Continue working in SS until work measures 16cm (6¼in), beginning and ending with a purl row.
next row: K2tog across the row [6 sts].
next row: P2tog and cast off across the row.

Legs

Make two.

For striped legs, work rows 1–4 in one colour, then change to the second colour on a knit row. Alternate between the colours, working a knit and a purl row in each one.

Cast on 3 sts.
row 1: knit, inc in each st [6 sts].
row 2: purl.
row 3: knit, inc in each st [12 sts].
Continue working in SS until work measures 26.5cm (10½in) from the tip of the toe, beginning and ending with a purl row.
Cast off purlwise.

Attaching the arms and legs

1. Pin the arms and legs inside out and back stitch up the long seam, leaving the top open for stuffing. Turn right-side out and stuff with small pieces of fibrefill (a paintbrush with a few stiff bristles works well). Do not over-stuff or the arms and legs will be fat and lumpy. Try to fill them evenly.

2. Sew the legs to the base of the body with whip stitch. Make sure the leg seam is towards the back of the doll.

3. Place the arms with the top of the arm at shoulder level. Mattress stitch all around the arm to attach it to the shoulder.

Needlesculpting the body

I like a shapely figure, especially on fashionable dolls like these. Knitted fabric lends itself extremely well to needlesculpting.

1. Take a tapestry needle threaded with the same colour yarn as the torso. Insert it at the base of the torso, take it up through the body and pass it back through a third of the way up the spine.

2. Take the thread back down the outside of the body to the initial insertion point and repeat the process. Pull the thread firmly to form the buttocks.

3. Insert the needle back into the body close to the point at which the thread came out through the spine, and pass it right through the torso to emerge at the belly button. Pass the needle back through the body and out again at the base of the torso, as close as possible to the first insertion point. Pull the thread taut, make a small holding stitch, and pass the thread back through the torso to neaten and snip it off.

4. If you wish to have a smaller or neater waist, then run a thread of body (or swimsuit) colour in and out of the stitches from centre back to centre front, in both directions. Make small, even stitches. Pull the waist thread firmly but not too tightly. Tie the ends together and neaten by passing the ends back into the body.

Needlesculpting the head

This is best done after the eyes and other features have been attached to the face.

1. Thread a tapestry needle with skin-coloured yarn and work in running stitch from the back of the head where it meets the neck, gently round the side of the head and under the chin area. Take the needle over no more than two stitches at a time. Your aim is to develop a slight chin which is lower than the base of the head (observe the back of a friend's head in relation to their chin).

2. Work the running stitches back around the other side of the head, matching the first side, and return to the point at which you started.

3. Pull the two ends of the thread firmly and tie a knot. Tidy up the loose ends by threading them back into the head. Trim off any excess threads.

Jenny

Jenny is a delicate blonde beauty. Her long wavy hair, pale skin and big blue eyes give her a romantic, dreamy look. To highlight her soft, feminine side, I have dressed her in a Spanish-style purple skirt and a purple and red halterneck top. Her matching purple ballet slippers are tied with pink ribbons that exactly match the tone of her pretty pink, rosebud lips. Around her neck she wears a pearl choker necklace, possibly given to her as a gift by one of her many admirers.

Making the body

Follow the instructions on pages 18–21 for making the body, and pages 12–14 for creating the face. Use the cream yarn for the skin and pink for the knitted-on swimsuit. For the face, use the small pair of blue eyes and the small pink lips provided as templates on pages 78–79. Jenny's nose is a single stitch made with a short length of the yarn used for her hair, and her fine eyebrows are carefully stitched on using back stitch worked in an arch over each eye.

For her hair, use the light beige textured yarn and follow the rooted method described on page 15. Add a short fringe using the same yarn.

materials

Needles: 3mm (US 3) and 4mm (US 6)

Crochet hook: 3mm (US 1 or C/D)

Yarns:

50g balls of yarn in cream for the body, pink for the knitted-on swimsuit, purple for the skirt and ballet slippers, and variegated purple and red for the halterneck top

light beige textured yarn for hair

Other materials:

half a pillow, or approx. 250g (9oz), of polyester fibrefill (you will probably use less)

old paintbrush for stuffing

either 3 empty toilet rolls or a piece of thick cardboard measuring 20 x 6cm (7¾ x 2¼in)

adhesive tape

tapestry needle

white felt for eyes, and pink felt for mouth

acrylic paints in brown, blue, black and white for painting the eyes

gloss acrylic varnish for sealing the eyes and making them shine

glue suitable for sticking felt to wool, e.g. PVA or a clear craft glue

50cm (19¾in) fine pink ribbon for the ballet slippers

short length of pearl trim for choker necklace

brown sewing thread for eyebrows

hook and eye for skirt fastening

Making up

Fold the skirt in half, right sides together. Mark 2cm (¾in) down from the waist. Back stitch from this point down along the centre back seam, including the frill. Neaten any loose threads and turn right-side out.

Sew a hook and eye to either side of the waist opening.

Halterneck top

Using 4mm (US 6) needles and variegated purple and red yarn, cast on 34 sts.

row 1: (K2, P2) to end of row.

row 2: (P2, K2) to end of row.

rows 3 and 4: repeat rows 1 and 2.

rows 5–13: SS for 9 rows, beginning and ending with a purl row.

row 14: K2tog, K to last 2 sts, K2tog [32 sts].

row 15: P2tog, P to last 2 sts, P2tog [30 sts].

rows 16–17: repeat rows 14 and 15 [26 sts].

row 18: K2tog, K9, K2tog twice, K9, K2tog [22 sts].

row 19: P2tog, P7, P2tog twice, P7, P2tog [18 sts].

row 20: K2tog, K6, K2tog, K6, K2tog [15 sts].

Turn and work on these stitches only.

row 21: P2tog, P4, P2tog.

row 22: K2tog, K2, K2tog.

row 23: P2tog twice.

Cast off.

Rejoin the yarn at other side and repeat rows 21–23.

Spanish-style skirt

Using 4mm (US 6) needles and purple yarn, cast on 120 sts.

rows 1–10: SS for 10 rows, ending with a purl row.

row 11: K2tog across the row [60 sts].

row 12: purl.

row 13: K2tog across the row [30 sts].

rows 14–28: SS for 15 rows, beginning and ending with a purl row.

row 29: knit, inc 1 st in every 6 to end [35 sts].

rows 30–40: SS for 10 rows, beginning and ending with a purl row.

row 41: knit, inc 1 st in every 5 to end [42 sts].

rows 42–56: SS for 15 rows, beginning and ending with a purl row.

row 57: (K4, K2tog) to end of row [35 sts].

row 58: (P5, P2tog) to end of row [30 sts].

Cast off knitwise.

To finish

Insert a crochet hook through one side of the top of the halterneck shaping. Crochet a tie approximately 10cm (4in) long. Repeat on the other side of the halterneck. Finish the ends of the ties with either threaded beads or a knot.
Fold the top in half, right sides together, and sew up the back seam. Turn right-side out.

If you do not wish to crochet the ties then you can knit them. For each tie, cast on one stitch and knit this for as many rows as you need to obtain the required length. Cast off and use the thread at the end of the tie to attach it to the halterneck top.

Ballet slippers

Make two.

Using 4mm (US 6) needles and purple yarn, cast on 3 sts.
row 1: knit, inc in every st [6 sts].
row 2: purl.
row 3: knit, inc in every st [12 sts].
row 4: purl.
row 5: knit, inc 1 st at each end of row [14 sts].
row 6: purl.
row 7: knit, inc 1 st at each end of row [16 sts].
rows 8–10: SS.
row 11: K6, K2tog.
Turn shoe and work on these 7 sts.
row 12: P2tog, purl to end.
row 13: K4, K2tog.
row 14: P2tog, purl to end.
Cast off knitwise.
Go back to the remaining stitches.
row 15: K2tog, K6.
row 16: P5, P2tog.
row 17: K2tog, K4.
row 18: P3, P2tog.
Cast off knitwise.

Making up

Fold each slipper in half, right sides together, and back stitch up the centre back seam. Turn right-side out. Cut the length of ribbon in half, one for each slipper. Fold each piece of ribbon in half and stitch it to the back of a slipper with a few tiny stitches.

tip

If the ribbon frays, either put a dot of fray stopper or craft glue on each end or, if it is an acrylic ribbon, melt the ends very slightly using a thread zapper.

Poppy

For this fun-loving, outgoing doll I have created a colourful outfit that goes perfectly with her dazzling personality. Poppy loves to party, and her brightly coloured mini dress and pink and purple hair mean she will definitely stand out in a crowd. For an added touch of glamour she has a faux feather boa draped casually around her shoulders, and a pair of black calf-length boots with a faux-fur trim make her long stripy legs look even longer. And for those long, summer days on the beach, Poppy wears a gorgeous purple bikini. This girl is certain to be the centre of attention wherever she goes.

Making the body

Follow the instructions on pages 18–21 for making the body, and pages 12–14 for creating the face. Use the dark brown yarn for the body, and follow the option for striped legs using the orange-red and dark purple yarn. For the face, use a small pair of blue eyes and small pink lips provided as templates on pages 78–79. Poppy's nose is a single stitch made with a short length of medium brown yarn, and the same yarn is used to embroider on her fine eyebrows using back stitch.

For her hair, use a soft, textured yarn in variegated pink and purple and follow the rooted method described on page 15.

materials

Needles: 3mm (US 3) and 4mm (US 6)

Crochet hook: 3mm (US 1 or C/D)

Yarns:

50g balls of yarn in dark brown for the body, orange-red and dark purple for the legs, purple for the bikini, black for the boots and multicoloured for the mini dress

variegated pink and purple soft, textured yarn for hair

Other materials:

half a pillow, or approx. 250g (9oz), of polyester fibrefill (you will probably use less)

old paintbrush for stuffing

either 3 empty toilet rolls *or* a piece of thick cardboard measuring 20 x 6cm (7¾ x 2¼in)

adhesive tape

tapestry needle

white felt for eyes, and pink felt for mouth

acrylic paints in brown, blue, black and white for painting the eyes

gloss acrylic varnish for sealing the eyes and making them shine

glue suitable for sticking felt to wool, e.g. PVA or a clear craft glue

short length of faux-fur trim for feather boa

short length of black fluffy yarn for edging boots

medium brown sewing thread for nose and eyebrows

Halterneck mini dress

Using 4mm (US 6) needles and multicoloured yarn, cast on 34 sts.
row 1: (K2, P2) to end of row.
row 2: (P2, K2) to end of row.
rows 3–8: repeat rows 1 and 2.
rows 9–33: SS, beginning and ending with a knit row.
row 34: P2tog, purl to last 2 sts, P2tog [32 sts].
row 35: K2tog, knit to last 2 sts, K2tog [30 sts].
rows 36–38: repeat rows 34 and 35 until 24 sts remain.
row 39: K2tog, K8, K2tog twice, K8, K2tog [20 sts].
row 40: P2tog, P6, P2tog.
Turn and work on these 8 sts only.
row 41: K2tog, K4, K2tog.
row 42: P2tog, P2, P2tog.
row 43: K2tog twice.
Cast off.
Rejoin the yarn and repeat rows 41–43.

To finish

1. With a crochet hook, join a length of yarn to the top of the halterneck on one side and crochet a tie 10cm (4in) long. Repeat on the other side of the dress. Finish off the ends of the ties with beads or simply tie in a knot.
2. Fold the dress in half with the right sides facing. Sew up the centre back seam. Turn right-side out.

If you prefer, knit the ties following the instructions on page 25.

Boots

Make two.

Using 4mm (US 6) needles and black yarn, cast on 3 sts.
row 1: knit, inc in every st across row [6 sts].
row 2: purl.
row 3: knit, inc in every st across row [12 sts].
row 4: purl.
row 5: knit, inc 1 st at each end of row [14 sts].
row 6: purl.
row 7: knit, inc 1 st at each end of row [16 sts].
Work in SS until work measures 10cm (4in).
Cut the yarn and join in the fancy yarn at beginning of next row.
rows 8–13: GS.
Cast off.

Making up

Fold the boot in half, right sides together. Back stitch along the side seam. Tie off and turn right-side out.

Bikini

Poppy is shown wearing her bikini on page 20.

Bottom

Begin at the waist.
Using 3mm (US 3) needles and purple yarn, cast on 24 sts.
rows 1–3: GS.
row 4: purl.
row 5: K2tog, knit to last 2 sts, K2tog [22 sts].
row 6: P2tog, purl to last 2 sts, P2tog [20 sts].
rows 7–10: repeat rows 5 and 6 until 12 sts remain.
rows 11–14: SS, beginning with a knit row and ending with a purl row.
row 15: knit, inc 1 st at each end of row [14 sts].
row 16: purl, inc 1 st at each end of row [16 sts].
rows 17–20: repeat rows 15 and 16 until 24 sts remain.
rows 21–23: GS.
Cast off purlwise.
Tidy up the loose yarn, turn inside out and sew the side seams with back stitch.

Top

Using 3mm (US 3) needles and purple yarn, cast on 24 sts.
row 1: knit.
row 2: purl.
row 3: K2tog twice, K16, K2tog twice [20 sts].
row 4: P2tog at each end of row [18 sts].
row 5: K2tog, K5, K2tog.
Turn and work back over these 7 sts only, leaving the remainder on the needle or a stitch holder.
row 6: purl.
row 7: K2tog, K3, K2tog [5 sts].
row 8: purl.
row 9: K2tog, K1, K2tog [3 sts].
Cast off purlwise.
Rejoin yarn and continue on the other set of stitches.
row 10: K2tog, K5, K2tog [7 sts].
row 11: purl.
row 12: K2tog, K3, K2tog [5 sts].
row 13: purl.
row 14: K2tog, K1, K2tog [3 sts].
Cast off purlwise.
Tidy up the loose ends.

To finish

1. Insert a 3mm (US 1 or C/D) crochet hook through the top stitch on the left-hand side of the bikini top. Crochet a length of yarn long enough for tying behind the neck. Make a similar tie on the other side of the bikini top.
2. Make similar straps for the sides of the bikini so they can be tied behind the back.

If you prefer, knit the ties following the instructions on page 25.

Ann

Ann is a nature lover, and is happiest when she is outdoors. She is a daydreamer, and her calm, contemplative moods set her apart from her friends. I have dressed her in a simple outfit that matches her lifestyle – a sweater, long skinny jeans that accentuate her beautiful long legs, a warm, stripy hat and pretty, yet practical purple shoes.

Making the body

Follow the instructions on pages 18–21 for making the body, and pages 12–14 for creating the face. Use the mid-brown yarn for the body and purple for the knitted-on swimsuit. For the face, use a small pair of blue eyes and small pink lips provided as templates on pages 78–79. Ann's nose is a single stitch made with a short length of dark brown yarn, and her eyebrows are made from slivers of brown felt cut out using the templates. I have also tinted this doll's eye area and cheeks (see page 14).

To create Ann's hair, I have used cheap, synthetic hair extensions, attached using the method described on page 15.

materials

Needles: 3mm (US 3) and 4mm (US 6)

Crochet hook: 3mm (US 1 or C/D)

Yarns:

50g balls of yarn in mid-brown for the body, purple for the knitted-on swimsuit and shoes, cream with coloured flecks for the sweater, black for the jeans, and blue, cream and beige for the hat

Other materials:

half a pillow, or approx. 250g (9oz), of polyester fibrefill (you will probably use less)

old paintbrush for stuffing

either 3 empty toilet rolls *or* a piece of thick cardboard measuring 20 x 6cm (7¾ x 2¼in)

adhesive tape

tapestry needle

white felt for eyes, and pink felt for mouth

acrylic paints in brown, blue, black and white for painting the eyes, and mauve and red for adding tints to the eye area and cheeks

gloss acrylic varnish for sealing the eyes and making them shine

glue suitable for sticking felt to wool, e.g. PVA or a clear craft glue

small scraps of brown felt for eyebrows

synthetic hair extensions and matching sewing thread

next row: purl.
next row: K11, K2tog, K12 [24 sts].
SS for 5 rows, beginning and ending with a purl row.
Cast off knitwise.

Making up

Put right sides together. Pin and back stitch the two seams. Re-fold the jeans so that you can sew a seam down each leg. Neaten the loose threads and turn right-side out.

Stripy hat

Using 4mm (US 6) needles and blue yarn, cast on 50 sts.
rows 1–10: GS.
Change to cream yarn.
row 11: knit.
row 12: purl.
Change to beige yarn and repeat rows 11 and 12.
Change to blue yarn and repeat rows 11 and 12.
Continue working stripes until there are 11 stripes in total.
rows 33–37: change back to blue yarn and GS for 5 rows.
row 38: K2tog across row [25 sts].
row 39: K2tog across row to last st, K1 [13 sts].
row 40: K2tog across row to last st, K1 [7 sts].
row 41: K2tog across row to last st, K1 [4 sts].
row 42: K2tog.
Cast off.

Making up

Fold the hat in half, right sides facing, and sew down the side seam. Neaten any loose ends and turn right-side out.

Skinny jeans

Make two.

Using 4mm (US 6) needles and black yarn, cast on 20 sts.
SS until work measures 24cm (9½in).
next row: knit, inc in first and last st [22 sts].
next row: purl, inc in first and last st [24 sts].
next row: knit, inc in first and last st [26 sts].
SS for 5 rows, beginning and ending with a purl row.
next row: K12, K2tog, K12 [25 sts].

Sweater

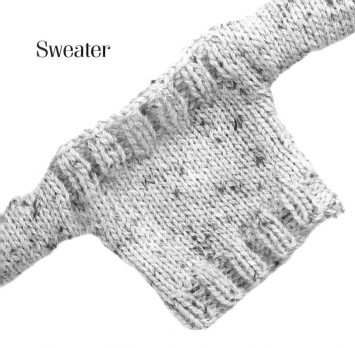

Using 4mm (US 6) needles and cream flecked yarn, cast on 24 sts.
rows 1–6: (K2, P2) to end (to make a rib).
rows 7–19: SS for 13 rows, beginning and ending with a purl row.

Sleeves

row 20: cast on 18 sts and knit to end (sleeve).
row 21: cast on 18 sts and purl to end (sleeve).
rows 22–26: SS.
row 27: P18 (sleeve), (K2, P2) for 24 sts (main body), P18 (sleeve).
row 28: K18 (sleeve), (K2, P2) for 24 sts (main body), K18 (sleeve).
rows 29–32: repeat rows 27 and 28.

Neck

row 33: K18, cast off 24 sts, K18.
row 34: P18.
Leave these sts on needle and go to other sleeve.
row 35: attach new yarn and cast on 24 sts.
Cut one of the threads of yarn and work with one thread only after sts are cast on. This will form the other side of the sweater.
row 36: return to the previous pattern of (K2, P2) for 24 sts across body of sweater, P18 to end of sleeve.
rows 37–41: K18, (K2, P2) for 24 sts, K18 (same as previous side).
row 42: knit across all sts.
row 43: purl across all sts.
Repeat rows 42 and 43 twice.
row 44: cast off 18 sts (sleeve), K23, cast off 18 sts (sleeve).
Rejoin yarn at body.

rows 45–57: SS for 14 rows, beginning with a purl row.
rows 58–63: (K2, P2) across body for 5 rows.
Cast off in K2, P2 rib.

Making up

With right sides together, pin along the sides and sleeves (the 'L' shape), sew with a back stitch, tuck in the loose ends and turn right-side out.

Shoes

Make two.

Using 3mm (US 3) needles and purple yarn, cast on 3 sts.
row 1: knit, inc in each st [6 sts].
row 2: purl.
row 3: knit, inc in each st [12 sts].
row 4: purl.
row 5: knit, inc 1 st at each end [14 sts].
row 6: purl.
row 7: knit, inc 1 st at each end [16 sts].
rows 8–10: SS.
row 11: K5, cast off 6 sts, K5.
Turn shoe and work on these 5 sts only.
rows 12–16: SS for 5 rows, beginning and ending with a purl row. Do not cast off. Cut yarn (leaving a long tail) and either leave sts on needle or transfer them to a stitch holder.
Return to other set of 5 sts and work as follows:
rows 17–20: SS for 4 rows.
row 21: cast on 6 sts and purl to end.
row 22: K11 then continue on the remaining 5 sts. (If sts are on a stitch holder, transfer them back to the needle.) You will now have a knitted row of 16 sts.
row 23: purl [16 sts].
row 24: Cast off knitwise.

Making up

Weave all loose strands into the knitting and trim, tightening any holes created by loose stitches as you work. Fold the shoe in half, right sides together, and back stitch up the back seam. Turn and the shoe is finished.

Here come the girls!

Willow, Samantha & Elaine

These three girls stand tall at approximately 59cm (23¼in) high, and are all knitted from the same pattern. Unlike the previous three dolls, the pattern for the front is different from that for the back, the face has a knitted-on, needlesculpted nose and the hands are given a thumb. These dolls are full of life and character, with a wardrobe to match. As before, all their clothes are interchangeable, and will also fit the other six dolls in the book.

Making the body

Body front

Using skin-coloured yarn, cast on 24 sts.
rows 1–12: SS, beginning with a knit row and ending with a purl row.

materials

Needles: 3mm (US 3)

Crochet hook: 3mm (US 1 or C/D)

Yarns:

1 x 50g ball of skin-coloured yarn and 1 x 50g ball of each coloured yarn for the striped legs

yarn (or synthetic hairpiece) for hair

Other materials:

half a pillow, or approx. 250g (9oz), of polyester fibrefill (you will probably use less)

old paintbrush for stuffing

either 3 empty toilet rolls *or* a piece of thick cardboard measuring 20 x 6cm (7¾ x 2¼in)

adhesive tape

tapestry needle

white felt for eyes, and pink or red felt for mouth

acrylic paints in brown, blue, black and white for painting the eyes

gloss acrylic varnish for sealing the eyes and making them shine

glue suitable for sticking felt to wool, e.g. PVA or a clear craft glue

Hips

row 13: K2tog, knit to last 2 sts, K2tog [22 sts].
row 14: purl.
rows 15–17: repeat rows 13–14 until there are 18 sts on the needle, ending with a knit row.

Waist

rows 18–24: SS for 7 rows, beginning and ending with a purl row.

Chest

row 25: knit, inc in first and last st [20 sts].
row 26: purl.
rows 27–29: repeat these 2 rows until there are 24 sts on the needle, ending with a knit row.
rows 30–38: SS for 9 rows, beginning and ending with a purl row.

Shoulders

row 39: K2tog, knit to last 2 sts, K2tog [22 sts].
row 40: P2tog, purl to last 2 sts, P2tog [20 sts].
rows 41–45: repeat these 2 rows until there are 10 sts on the needle, ending with a knit row.

Neck

rows 46–52: SS for 7 rows, beginning and ending with a purl row.

Lower part of head

row 53: knit, inc in first and last st [12 sts].
row 54: purl.
row 55: K4, inc in each of next 4 sts, K4 [16 sts].
row 56: purl.
row 57: K5, inc in each of next 6 sts, K5 [22 sts].
row 58: purl.
row 59: knit, inc in first and last st [24 sts].
row 60: purl.
row 61: knit, inc in first and last st [26 sts].
rows 62–68: SS.

Nose

row 69: K12, inc in each of next 2 sts, K12 [28 sts].
rows 70–72: SS.
row 73: K12, K2tog twice, K12 [26 sts].

Forehead

rows 74–78: SS for 5 rows, beginning and ending with a purl row.

Top of head

row 79: K2tog, K to last 2 sts, K2tog [24 sts].
row 80: purl.
rows 81–94: repeat rows 79 and 80 until 10 sts remain.
Cast off knitwise.

Body back

Follow instructions for Body Front up to row 52.

row 53: knit, inc in first and last st [12 sts].
row 54: purl.
row 55: knit, inc in first and last st [14 sts].
row 56: purl.
row 57: (K1, inc in next st) to end of row [21 sts].
row 58: purl.
row 59: inc in first st, K9, inc next st, K9, inc in last st [24 sts].
rows 60–74: SS for 15 rows, beginning and ending with a purl row.
row 75: K2tog, knit to last 2 sts, K2tog [22 sts].
row 76: purl.
rows 77–87: repeat rows 75 and 76 until 10 sts remain. Cast off purlwise.

Making up

1. Pin the body front and body back together with right sides facing. Ease together the front and back of the head.

2. Sew the front and back of the doll together using back stitch leaving the bottom end open for stuffing. Turn right-side out.

3. Stuff a small amount of polyester fibrefill up into the top of the head. Insert a toilet-roll backbone into the body and up into neck (see page 19). Gradually add stuffing around the backbone and fill the head. Put a small ball of stuffing into the knitted nose area. Fill out the cheeks and chin. Only put the smallest amount of stuffing into the neck, to just cover the backbone.

4. Fill the rest of the body firmly but without over-stuffing.

5. Whip stitch the bottom opening closed.

Arms

Make two.

Cast on 3 sts.
row 1: knit, inc in each st [6 sts].
row 2: purl.
row 3: knit, inc in each st [12 sts].
row 4: purl.
row 5: (K1, inc in next st) to end of row [18 sts].
rows 6–12: SS for 7 rows, beginning and ending with a purl row.

Thumb

row 13: knit, inc in first and last st [20 sts].
row 14: purl, inc in first and last st [22 sts].
row 15: knit, inc in first and last st [24 sts].
rows 16–18: SS, beginning and ending with a purl row.
row 19: cast off 5 sts knitwise at beginning of row, knit to end [19 sts].
row 20: cast off 5 sts purlwise at beginning of row, purl to end [14 sts].
row 21: K2tog, knit to last 2 sts, K2tog [12 sts].
SS until work measures 16cm (6¼in) from tip.
next row: K2tog, knit to last 2 sts, K2tog [10 sts].
next row: P2tog, purl to last 2 sts, P2tog [8 sts].
next row: K2tog 4 times.
next row: P2tog twice and cast off.

Making up

1. Fold the arms in half, with the right sides facing. Line up the thumbs, pin and sew from the fingertips to the top of the arm, leaving the last 1cm (½in) open for stuffing.

2. Turn the arms right-side out. Stuff gently, and not too much.

3. Place the open end on the doll's body at shoulder level and join the armhole to the shoulder using mattress stitch.

Legs

Make two.

This pattern is for striped legs in two colours. If you want plain legs, follow the same instructions but ignore the colour changes.

Using the foot colour, cast on 3 sts.
row 1: knit, inc in each st [6 sts].
row 2: purl.
row 3: knit, inc in each st [12 sts].
row 4: purl.
row 5: knit, inc in each st [24 sts].
rows 6–18: SS for 13 rows, beginning and ending with a purl row.
row 19: K6, (K2tog) six times, K6 [18 sts].
row 20: purl.
Change colour for first stripe.
row 21: knit.
row 22: purl.
Change colour again for second stripe.

rows 23–24: repeat rows 21 and 22.
Continue working stripes in SS until work measures 29cm (11½in) from tip.
Cast off purlwise.

tip
You can use as many different colours as you like for the stripes. Each colour change must be made on a knit row.

Making up

1. Fold each leg in half with right sides facing. Pin and back stitch from the toe to the top edge opening. Make sure the stripes are aligned before stitching.

2. Turn right-side out and fill with small amounts of stuffing.

3. Pin the legs to the base of the torso and whip stitch each leg to the body.

Needlesculpting the body and head

Follow the instructions provided on page 21 for Jenny, Poppy and Ann.

Sculpting the nose

1. Using a tapestry needle and a length of skin-coloured yarn, insert the needle into the back of the head or neck and bring it out at one side of the bridge of the nose.

2. Push the needle into the stuffing and bring it out on the opposite side of the nose, passing the thread under the stuffing. Pull the thread gently; too much, and the nose will distort.

3. Repeat step 2, taking the thread back to the other side of the nose, where you started.

4. To shape the nostrils, push the needle down through the nose and bring it out through the underside of the nose, just to one side. Make a small stitch and bring the needle back through close to where it went in. Pull the thread gently. Repeat on the other side for the second nostril.

5. Take the needle and thread back out through the back of the neck or head and snip off the excess thread.

Sculpt the rest of the face following the method explained on page 13.

Willow

With her long auburn hair, blue eyes and red lips contrasting dramatically with her pale, ivory skin, Willow is a stunning Celtic beauty. Though she appears cool and sophisticated in her black top, grey mini skirt and fashionable black coat, her fiery, untamed mane of hair suggests a girl with a wild spirit.

Making the body

Follow the instructions on pages 36–39 for making the body using pale cream yarn, and pages 12–14 for creating the face. For the face, use a large pair of blue eyes and small red lips provided as templates on pages 78–79. Willow's eyebrows are stitched on using mid-brown sewing thread. I have also tinted this doll's eye area using purple acrylic paint, and given her pink cheeks (see page 14). For her soft, fine hair, I have used a soft, textured yarn, and stitched it on to her head densely using the rooted method (see page 15). Leave her hair long and add a short fringe using the same yarn.

materials

Needles: 3mm (US 3) and 4mm (US 6)

Crochet hook: 3mm (US 1 or C/D)

Yarns:

50g balls of yarn in pale cream for the body, three shades of purple for the legs, black for the off-the-shoulder top, grey and purple for the skirt, pink for her underwear, and a flecked black yarn for the coat

soft, textured yarn suitable for hair in golden brown/auburn

Other materials:

half a pillow, or approx. 250g (9oz), of polyester fibrefill (you will probably use less)

old paintbrush for stuffing

either 3 empty toilet rolls or a piece of thick cardboard measuring 20 x 6cm (7¾ x 2¼in)

adhesive tape

tapestry needle

white felt for eyes, and red felt for mouth

acrylic paints in brown, blue, black and white for painting the eyes, and purple and red for adding tints to the eye area and cheeks

gloss acrylic varnish for sealing the eyes and making them shine

glue suitable for sticking felt to wool, e.g. PVA or a clear craft glue

mid-brown sewing thread for eyebrows

three press-studs

Off-the-shoulder top

Bodice

Using 4mm (US 6) needles and black yarn, cast on 36 sts.
row 1: (K1, P1) to end of row.
row 2: (P1, K1) to end of row.
rows 3–4: repeat rows 1 and 2.
SS until work measures 7cm (2¾in), beginning and ending with a purl row.
Cast off knitwise.

Sleeves

Make two.

Cast on 20 sts.
row 1: (K1, P1) to end of row.
row 2: (P1, K1) to end of row.
rows 3–4: repeat rows 1 and 2.
SS for 9 rows, beginning and ending with a purl row.
Cast off knitwise.

Making up

1. Fold the bodice in half lengthwise, right sides together. Back stitch up the centre back seam. Turn right-side out.

2. Fold each sleeve in half, right sides together. Sew up the seam. Turn each sleeve right-side out.

3. Attach a sleeve to each side of the bodice. Place the sleeve seam at the top of the bodice and secure it with a few stitches.

tip

This top is very close fitting and is best pulled up over the doll's legs rather than down over her head.

Underwear

Using 3mm (US 3) needles and pink yarn, cast on 24 sts.
rows 1–3: GS.
rows 4–6: SS, beginning and ending with a purl row.
row 7: K2tog, knit to last 2 sts, K2tog [22 sts].
row 8: P2tog, purl to last 2 sts, P2tog [20 sts].
rows 9–16: repeat rows 7 and 8 until 4 sts remain.
rows 17–20: SS for 4 rows, beginning with a knit row and ending with a purl row.
row 21: knit, inc in first and last st [6 sts].
row 22: purl, inc in first and last st [8 sts].
rows 23–30: repeat rows 21 and 22 until there are 24 sts on the needle.
rows 31–34: SS for 4 rows, beginning and ending with a knit row.
row 35: knit.
Cast off knitwise.

Making up

Fold the panties in half, right sides facing. Back stitch the small side seams. Neaten any loose ends and turn right-side out. If you wish, chain stitch a simple daisy design on to the pants in contrasting colours.

Mini skirt

Using 4mm (US 6) needles and grey yarn, cast on 60 sts.
row 1: (K1, P1) to end of row.
row 2: (P1, K1) to end of row.
rows 3–4: repeat rows 1 and 2.
rows 5–7: SS, beginning and ending with a purl row.
rows 8–9: change to purple yarn and SS for two rows.
row 10: (K1 grey, K2 purple) to end of row.
row 11: (P2 purple, P1 grey) to end of row.
rows 12–15: SS in grey yarn, beginning with a knit row.
row 16: (K1 grey, K3 purple) to end of row.
row 17: (P3 purple, P1 grey) to end of row.
Change to grey yarn.
rows 18–25: SS for 8 rows, beginning with a knit row and
ending with a purl row.
row 26: K2tog, knit to last 2 sts, K2tog [58 sts].
row 27: purl.
row 28: K2tog to end of row [29 sts].
Cast off purlwise.

Making up

Fold the skirt in half, right sides together. Put a pin 2cm
(¾in) down from the waistband. Sew the seam from here
to the hem of the skirt. Neaten any loose ends. Turn right-
side out and sew a press-stud on to the waist opening.

Coat

Back

Using 4mm (US 6) needles and flecked black yarn, cast on 50 sts.
rows 1–9: GS.
SS, beginning and ending with a purl row, until work measures 21cm (8¼in).
next row: K2tog to end of row [25 sts].
SS for 15 rows, beginning and ending with a purl row.
next row: K2tog, knit to last 2 sts, K2tog [23 sts].
next row: P2tog, purl to last 2 sts, P2tog [21 sts].
Repeat last 2 rows until 13 sts remain.
Cast off knitwise.

Left front

Cast on 26 sts.
rows 1–9: GS.
row 10: K6, purl to end of row.
row 11: knit.
Repeat rows 10 and 11 until work measures 21cm (8¼in) from the hem. End with a purl row.
next row: K2tog to end of row [13 sts].
next row: K6, purl to end of row.
next row: knit.
Repeat last 2 rows 13 times.
next row: K6, P5, P2tog [12 sts].
next row: K2tog, K10 [11 sts].

next row: K6, P3, P2tog [10 sts].
next row: K2tog, K8 [9 sts].
next row: K6, P1, P2tog [8 sts].
next row: K2tog, K6 [7 sts].
Cast off knitwise.

Right front

Cast on 26 sts.
rows 1–9: GS.
row 10: purl to last 6 sts, K6.
row 11: knit.
Repeat rows 10 and 11 until work measures 21cm (8¼in) from hem. End with a purl row.
next row: K2tog to end of row [13 sts].
next row: purl to last 6 sts, K6.
next row: knit.
Repeat last 2 rows 13 times.
next row: P2tog, purl to last 6 sts, K6 [12 sts].
next row: K2tog, knit to end [11 sts].
next row: P2tog, purl to last 6 sts, K6 [10 sts].
next row: K2tog, knit to end [9 sts].
next row: P2tog, purl to last 6 sts, K6 [8 sts].
next row: K2tog, knit to end [7 sts].
Cast off knitwise.

Sleeves

Make two.

Cast on 30 sts.
rows 1–9: GS.
row 10: purl.
row 11: K2tog, knit to last 2 sts, K2tog [28 sts].
row 12: purl.
Repeat rows 11 and 12 until 24 sts remain.
SS until work measures 14cm (5½in).
Cast off purlwise.

Making up

1. Place the back right-side up. Place the left front and the right front on top, right sides down. Sew across the shoulder seams.

2. Sew the side seams from the hem of the coat up to 0.5cm (¼in) above the waistline. Turn the coat right-side out.

3. Fold each sleeve in half lengthwise and sew up the seam. Turn them right-side out.

4. Put the top of a sleeve in one of the armholes, matching the side seam of the coat with the sleeve seam. Ease the sleeve in place and stitch in place on the inside. Repeat for the other sleeve.

5. Neaten any loose ends.

6. Sew on two press-studs, one at the neck and one at the waist.

Samantha

Samantha loves to keep fit, and has a simple, comfortable outfit to match her active lifestyle. Her blue baggy pants and matching crop top provide a stunning contrast to her eye-catching, bright red head of hair. To add a touch of sparkle to her outfit, I have added a string of coloured sequins around her neck.

Making the body

Follow the instructions on pages 36–39 for making the body using brown yarn, and give her stripy lilac and blue legs. Follow the instructions on pages 12–14 for creating the face, using a large pair of brown eyes and a set of red lips provided as templates on pages 78–79. Samantha's eyebrows are stitched on using dark brown sewing thread, and I have tinted the eye area and cheeks using brown and red acrylic paint (see page 14). For her hair, I have used a soft, chunky textured red yarn that gives the appearance of thick hair, and stitched it on to her head using the rooted method (see page 15).

materials

Needles: 3mm (US 3) and 4mm (US 6)

Crochet hook: 3mm (US 1 or C/D)

Yarns:

50g balls of yarn in brown for the body, blue and lilac for the legs, and blue for the pants and crop top

soft, textured red yarn for hair

Other materials:

half a pillow, or approx. 250g (9oz), of polyester fibrefill (you will probably use less)

old paintbrush for stuffing

either 3 empty toilet rolls *or* a piece of thick cardboard measuring 20 x 6cm (7¾ x 2¼in)

adhesive tape

tapestry needle

white felt for eyes, and red felt for mouth

acrylic paints in brown, black and white for painting the eyes, and dark brown and red for adding tints to the eye area and cheeks

gloss acrylic varnish for sealing the eyes and making them shine

glue suitable for sticking felt to wool, e.g. PVA or a clear craft glue

dark brown sewing thread for eyebrows

string of multicoloured sequins for choker necklace

Baggy pants

Make two pieces.

Using 4mm (US 6) needles and blue yarn, cast on 28 sts.
rows 1–5: GS.
SS, beginning with a knit row and ending with a purl row, until work measures 17cm (6¾in). For longer pants, continue in SS until they are the desired length.
next 2 rows: K2tog, knit to last 2 sts, K2tog [26 sts].
GS for 3 rows.
Cast off knitwise.

Making up

Place the two pieces right sides together and back stitch the seam around the body starting at the waist. Fold each leg in half lengthways and sew up the seams. Neaten any loose ends and turn right-side out.

Long-sleeved crop top

Sleeves

Make two.

Using 4mm (US 6) needles and blue yarn, cast on 48 sts.
rows 1–3: GS.
rows 4–7: SS, starting with a purl row and ending with a knit row.
row 8: K2tog, knit to last 2 sts, K2tog [28 sts].
row 9: knit.
row 10: K2tog, knit to last 2 sts, K2tog [26 sts].
row 11: knit.
row 12: purl.
row 13: K2tog, knit to last 2 sts, K2tog [24 sts].
rows14–16: SS, beginning and ending with a purl row.
Repeat rows 13–16 until 18 sts remain.
SS for 10 rows, ending with a knit row.
Cast off purlwise.

Back

Cast on 30 sts.
rows 1–3: GS.
rows 4–7: SS, beginning with a purl row and ending with a knit row.
rows 8–10: GS.

row 11: K2tog, knit to last 2 sts, K2tog [28 sts].
row 12: purl.
row 13: K2tog, knit to last 2 sts, K2tog [26 sts].
rows 14–18: SS, beginning and ending with a purl row.
row 19: K2tog, knit to last 2 sts, K2tog [24 sts].
row 20: P2tog, purl to last 2 sts, P2tog [22 sts].
rows 21–24: repeat rows 19 and 20 until 14 sts remain.
Cast off knitwise.

Front

Cast on 30 sts.
rows 1–3: GS.
rows 4–7: SS, beginning with a purl row and ending with
a knit row.
rows 8–10: GS.
row 11: K2tog, knit to last 2 sts, K2tog [28 sts].
row 12: purl.
row 13: K2tog, knit to last 2 sts, K2tog [26 sts].
row 14: purl.
row 15: K13, turn and work on these sts only.
rows 16–18: SS, beginning and ending with a purl row.
row 19: K2tog, knit to end.
row 20: purl to last 2 sts, P2tog.
rows 21–22: repeat rows 19 and 20.
row 23: K2tog, knit to last 2 sts, K2tog.
row 24: P2tog twice.
Cast off.
Rejoin for other side and repeat rows 16 onwards.

Making up

1. Place the back and front together with right sides facing. Back stitch them together at the shoulder seams. Pin and sew the side seams up to the end of the second band of garter stitch. Keep inside out.

2. Fold each sleeve in half, right sides together, and sew along the length of each sleeve. Turn the sleeves right-side out. Place the sleeves in the armholes, pin and stitch, making sure the sleeve seams are lined up with the side seams. Turn right-side out.

Elaine

This girl is bursting with personality, and has an outfit to match! Knitted in dazzling, multicoloured eyelash yarn, her wrap-around skirt is tied at the waist with a cord decorated with beads. Her matching pink cape, which she wears over a cream strappy top, is edged with the same yarn. On her head she wears a striking pink hat with a fluffy multicoloured trim, creating a stunning contrast with her long, black curly hair and dark skin. Her outfit is completed with a cream-coloured bag, again trimmed with pink, purple and yellow fluffy yarn.

Making the body

Follow the instructions on pages 36–39 for making the body. Use dark brown yarn and add pink and purple striped legs. See pages 12–14 for creating the face. Use a large pair of brown eyes and pink lips from the templates provided on pages 78–79. This doll has no eyebrows, but I have added a subtle pink tint to her cheeks. For her hair, I have used a soft, textured black yarn that resembles dreadlocks, and stitched it on to her head densely using the rooted method (see page 15).

materials

Needles: 3mm (US 3), 4mm (US 6) and 10mm (US 15)

Crochet hook: 3mm (US 1 or C/D)

Yarns:

50g balls of yarn in dark brown for the body, purple and pink for the legs, cream for the strappy top and bag, pink for the cape, hat and underwear, multicoloured eyelash yarn and/or fluffy novelty yarn in pastel shades for the skirt and edging on the cape, bag and hat, and untextured multicoloured yarn for the top of the skirt and the ties

soft, textured black yarn suitable for hair

Other materials:

half a pillow, or approx. 250g (9oz), of polyester fibrefill (you will probably use less)

old paintbrush for stuffing

either 3 empty toilet rolls *or* a piece of thick cardboard measuring 20 x 6cm (7¾ x 2¼in)

adhesive tape

tapestry needle

white felt for eyes, and pink felt for mouth

acrylic paints in brown, black and white for painting the eyes, and red for adding a light tint to the cheeks

gloss acrylic varnish for sealing the eyes and making them shine

glue suitable for sticking felt to wool, e.g. PVA or a clear craft glue

coloured beads for decorating skirt ties

Wrap-around skirt

Using the multicoloured eyelash (or other fluffy) yarn and 10mm (US 15) needles, cast on 60 sts.
rows 1–10: GS.
Change to untextured multicoloured yarn and 4mm (US 6) needles.
rows 11–13: SS, beginning and ending with a purl row.
row 14: K2tog across the row [30 sts].
Cast off knitwise.

To finish

1. Crochet two ties, each 10cm (4in) long, from each side of the skirt. Add some beads to decorate.

2. Crochet two loops, each approximately 3cm (1¼in) long, 1cm (½in) in from each side of the skirt. Thread the ties through the loops when your doll is dressed and use them to pull the skirt together to the desired fit.

3. Add some decorative trims, threaded with beads, and tie them round the loops to embellish the top of the skirt.

If you prefer, knit the ties and loops by knitting into a single stitch until the desired length is reached (see page 25).

Cape

Using 10mm (US 15) needles and eyelash (or other fluffy) yarn, cast on 60 sts.
rows 1–4: GS.
row 5: K2tog across the row [30 sts].
Change to 4mm (US 6) needles and untextured yarn.
rows 6–8: SS, beginning and ending with a purl row.
row 9: K2tog across the row [15 sts].
rows 10–12: SS, beginning and ending with a purl row.
row 13: cast off knitwise.
Crochet or knit ties for each side of neck of cape.

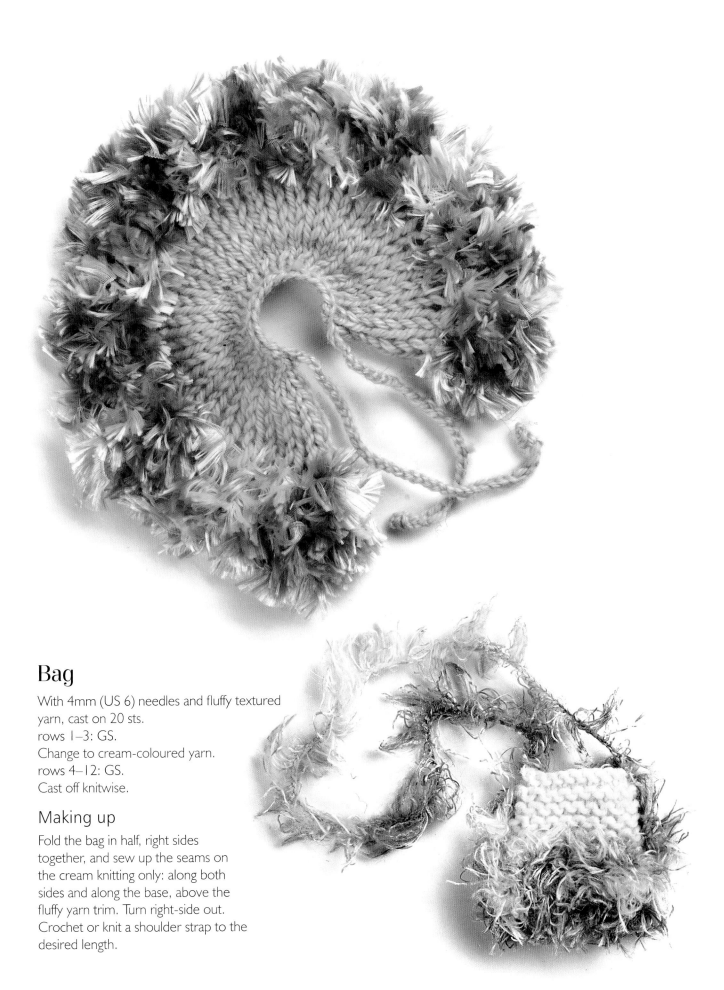

Bag

With 4mm (US 6) needles and fluffy textured yarn, cast on 20 sts.
rows 1–3: GS.
Change to cream-coloured yarn.
rows 4–12: GS.
Cast off knitwise.

Making up

Fold the bag in half, right sides together, and sew up the seams on the cream knitting only: along both sides and along the base, above the fluffy yarn trim. Turn right-side out. Crochet or knit a shoulder strap to the desired length.

Hat

With fluffy textured yarn and 4mm (US 6) needles, cast on 44 sts.
rows 1–3: GS.
Change to pink yarn.
rows 4–27: SS, beginning with a knit row and ending with a purl row.
row 28: K9, K2tog twice, K18, K2tog twice, K9.
rows 29–31: SS.
row 32: K9, inc in each of next 2 sts, K18, inc in each of next 2 sts, K9.
rows 33–40: SS.
Cast off purlwise.

Making up

1. Fold the hat in half lengthwise, right sides facing. Back stitch from the bottom to the top. Neaten off the thread.

2. Re-fold the hat so that the seam is now at the centre back. Back stitch along the top seam. Neaten the thread and turn right-side out.

tip

This hat will not fit a doll with great masses of hair. You can make it bigger by increasing the stitches by a multiple of two. Add half the total number of extra stitches added to each end of rows 28 and 32, so if you added four stitches, row 28 would become: K11, K2tog twice, K18, K2tog twice, K11, and similarly for row 32.

Underwear

Using 3mm (US 3) needles and pink yarn, cast on 24 sts.
rows 1–3: GS.
rows 4–6: SS, beginning and ending with a purl row.
row 7: K2tog, knit to last 2 sts, K2tog [22 sts].
row 8: P2tog, purl to last 2 sts, P2tog [20 sts].
rows 9–16: repeat rows 7 and 8 until 4 sts remain.
rows 17–20: SS for 4 rows, beginning with a knit row and ending with a purl row.
row 21: knit, inc in first and last st [6 sts].
row 22: purl, inc in first and last st [8 sts].
rows 23–30: repeat rows 21 and 22 until there are 24 sts on the needle.
rows 31–34: SS for 4 rows, beginning and ending with a knit row.
row 35: knit.
Cast off knitwise.

Making up

Fold the panties in half, right sides facing. Back stitch the small side seams. Neaten any loose ends and turn right-side out. If you wish, chain stitch a simple daisy design on to the pants in contrasting colours.

Strappy top

Using cream yarn and 4mm (US 6) needles, cast on
36 sts.

row 1: (K1, P1) to end of row.
row 2: (P1, K1) to end of row.
rows 3–4: repeat rows 1 and 2.
SS until work measures 7cm (2¾in), beginning and ending
with a purl row.
Cast off knitwise.
Crochet two cords, each approximately 5cm (2in) long.

If you prefer, knit the cords following the instructions on
page 25.

Making up

1. Fold the piece in half lengthwise, right sides together.
   Back stitch up the centre back seam. Turn right-
   side out.
2. Adjust the straps on the doll and stitch
   them in the desired place.

Magic in the air

Miranda, Rose & Chloe

These three girls are approximately 59cm (23¼in) high, and are all knitted from the same pattern. Unlike the previous dolls, the head is knitted in two separate parts that are then joined together. This gives a larger, more shapely head with a more pronounced chin. Once more, I have given each doll her own special character, though of course you are free to adapt and modify the designs to create a special doll of your own. All their clothes are interchangeable, and will also fit the other six dolls in the book.

Making the body

Body front and back

Make two.

Using 3mm (US 3) needles and skin-coloured yarn, cast on 24 sts.
rows 1–14: SS, beginning with a knit row and ending with a purl row.

Hips

row 15: K2tog, knit to last 2 sts, K2tog [22 sts].
row 16: P2tog, purl to last 2 sts, P2tog [20 sts].
row 17: repeat row 15 [18 sts].

Waist

rows 18–20: SS, beginning and ending with a purl row.

Chest

row 21: knit, inc in first and last st [20 sts].
row 22: purl.
rows 23–25: repeat rows 21 and 22 until there are 24 sts.
rows 26–40: SS, beginning and ending with a purl row.

Shoulders

row 41: K2tog, knit to last 2 sts, K2tog [22 sts].
row 42: P2tog, purl to last 2 sts, P2tog [20 sts].
rows 43–47: repeat rows 41 and 42 until 10 sts remain.

Neck

rows 48–66: SS.
Cast off knitwise.

Head front

Cast on 3 sts.
row 1: inc in each st [6 sts].
row 2: purl.
row 3: inc in each st [12 sts].
row 4: purl.
row 5: knit, inc in first st, K3, inc in each of next 4 sts, K3, inc in last st [18 sts].
row 6: purl.
row 7: K5, inc in each of next 8 sts, K5 [26 sts].

materials

Needles: 3mm (US 3)
Crochet hook: 3mm (US 1 or C/D)
Yarns:
1 x 50g ball of skin-coloured yarn and 1 x 50g ball of each coloured yarn for the striped legs
yarn (or synthetic hairpiece) for hair
Other materials:
half a pillow, or approx. 250g (9oz), of polyester fibrefill (you will probably use less)
old paintbrush for stuffing
either 3 empty toilet rolls or a piece of thick cardboard measuring 20 x 6cm (7¾ x 2¼in)
adhesive tape
tapestry needle
white felt for eyes, and pink or red felt for mouth
acrylic paints in brown, blue, black and white for painting the eyes
gloss acrylic varnish for sealing the eyes and making them shine
glue suitable for sticking felt to wool, e.g. PVA or a clear craft glue

row 8: purl.
row 9: knit, inc in first and last st [28 sts].
rows 10–18: SS, beginning and ending with a purl row.

Nose

row 19: K13, inc in each of next 2 sts, K13 [30 sts].
rows 20–22: SS, ending with a purl row.
row 23: inc in first st, K12, K2tog twice, K12, inc in last st [30 sts].
row 24: purl.
row 25: knit, inc in first and last st [32 sts].
rows 26–34: SS.
row 35: K2tog, knit to last 2 sts, K2tog [30 sts].
row 36: purl.
rows 37–42: repeat rows 35 and 36 [24 sts].
row 43: K2tog across the row [12 sts].
Cast off purlwise.

Head back

Cast on 10 sts.
row 1: knit, inc in each st [20 sts].
row 2: purl.
row 3: knit, inc in first and last st [22 sts].
row 4: purl.
rows 5–9: repeat rows 3 and 4 until 28 sts on needle, ending with a knit row.
rows 10–30: SS for 21 rows, beginning and ending with a purl row.
row 31: K2tog, knit to last 2 sts, K2tog [26 sts].
row 32: purl.
rows 33–34: repeat rows 31 and 32 [24 sts].
row 35: K2tog across row [12 sts].
Cast off purlwise.

Making up

1. Place the body pieces with right sides together, pin and sew down each side seam using back stitch. Leave the neck and base open. Turn right-side out.

2. Place both head pieces with right sides together. Match the tops and sides of the head. Pin, and sew from one side of the head to the other. Turn right-side out.

3. Stuff the top of the head with small pieces of polyester fibrefill. Insert a toilet-roll backbone into the head. Stuff the rest of the head, filling out the nose area, cheeks and chin.

4. Pull the body up over the cardboard backbone, until the end of the neck goes into the head. Pin the head to the neck.

5. Lightly stuff the neck, just enough to cover the cardboard backbone. Continue to fill the shoulders and the rest of the body.

6. Using mattress stitch, sew the head to the neck. Whip stitch the bottom opening closed.

Arms

Make two.

Cast on 3 sts.
row 1: inc in each st [6 sts].
row 2: purl.
row 3: inc in each st [12 sts].
row 4: purl.
row 5: (K1, inc in next st) across row [18 sts].
rows 6–12: SS, beginning and ending with a purl row.

Thumb

row 13: knit, inc in first and last st [20 sts].
row 14: purl, inc in first and last st [22 sts].
row 15: knit, inc in first and last st [24 sts].
rows 16–18: SS, beginning and ending with a purl row.
row 19: cast off 5 sts at beginning of row, knit to end [19 sts].
row 20: cast off 5 sts at beginning of row, purl to end [14 sts].
row 21: K2tog, knit to last 2 sts, K2tog [12 sts].
SS until work measures 16cm (6¼in) from the tip.
next row: K2tog, knit to last 2 sts, K2tog [10 sts].
next row: P2tog, purl to last 2 sts, P2tog [8 sts].
next row: K2tog 4 times.
next row: P2tog twice.
Cast off.

Making up

1. Fold the arms in half, with the right sides facing. Line up the thumbs, pin and sew from the fingertips to the top of the arm, leaving the last 1cm (½in) open for stuffing.

2. Turn the arms right-side out. Stuff gently, and not too much.

3. Place the open end on the doll's body at shoulder level and join the armhole to the shoulder using mattress stitch.

Legs

Make two.

With the foot colour, cast on 3 sts.
row 1: knit, inc in each st [6 sts].
row 2: purl.
row 3: knit, inc in each st [12 sts].
row 4: purl.
row 5: knit, inc in each st [24 sts].
rows 6–18: SS, beginning and ending with a purl row.
row 19: K6, K2tog six times, K6 [18 sts].
row 20: purl.
Change colour for first stripe.
row 21: knit.
row 22: purl.
Change colour for second stripe. Repeat rows 20 and 21. Continue working stripes in SS until work measures 29cm (11½in) from tip.
Cast off purlwise.

Making up

1. Fold each leg in half with right sides facing. Pin and back stitch from the toe to the top edge opening.

2. Turn right-side out and fill with small amounts of stuffing.

3. Pin the legs to the base of the torso and whip stitch each leg to the body.

tip

You can use as many different colours as you like for the stripes. Each colour change must be made on a knit row. If your doll has plain legs, ignore the colour changes.

Needlesculpting the body and head

Follow the instructions provided on page 21 for Jenny, Poppy and Ann.

Needlesculpting the nose

1. Using a tapestry needle and a length of skin-coloured yarn, insert the needle into the back of the head or neck and bring it out at one side of the bridge of the nose.

2. Push the needle into the stuffing and bring it out on the opposite side of the nose, passing the thread under the stuffing. Pull the thread gently; too much, and the nose will distort.

3. Repeat step 2, taking the thread back to the other side of the nose, where you started.

4. To shape the nostrils, push the needle down through the nose and bring it out through the underside of the nose, just to one side. Make a small stitch and bring the needle back through close to where it went in. Pull the thread gently. Repeat on the other side for the second nostril.

5. Take the needle and thread back out through the back of the neck or head and snip off the excess thread.

Sculpt the rest of the face following the method explained on page 13.

Miranda

The stylish Miranda takes her inspiration from the 1960s, when mini dresses were all the rage. Here she teams her pink and purple mini with a yellow-green waistcoat, a button tie-belt and a multicoloured beret. With her bright pink hair, the end result is definitely psychedelic!

Making the body

Follow the instructions on pages 58–61 for making the body using cream yarn, and pages 12–14 for creating the face. Use a large pair of blue eyes and pink lips, provided as templates on pages 78–79. Miranda's eyebrows are cut from brown felt, using the templates provided, and I have tinted her eye area and cheeks using purple and pink acrylic paint (see page 14). For her hair, I have used a pink, nylon hairpiece that I unstitched to form a long strip of hair. I wrapped the strip round and round the doll's head and secured it with stitches (see page 15). I then cut the hair to the length shown, leaving the front sections long – these I wound together into braids.

materials

Needles: 3mm (US 3), 4mm (US 6) and 10mm (US 15)

Crochet hook: 3mm (US 1 or C/D)

Yarns:

50g balls of yarn in cream for the body, blue, beige and white for the legs, blue for the underwear, variegated pink and purple for the dress, yellow-green for the waistcoat, black for the choker necklace and belt, and multicoloured fluffy yarn for the beret

Other materials:

half a pillow, or approx. 250g (9oz), of polyester fibrefill (you will probably use less)

old paintbrush for stuffing

either 3 empty toilet rolls or a piece of thick cardboard measuring 20 x 6cm (7¾ x 2¼in)

adhesive tape

tapestry needle

white felt for eyes, and pink felt for mouth

acrylic paints in brown, blue, black and white for painting the eyes, and purple and red for adding tints to the eye area and cheeks

gloss acrylic varnish for sealing the eyes and making them shine

glue suitable for sticking felt to wool, e.g. PVA or a clear craft glue

brown felt for eyebrows

bright pink synthetic hairpiece or hair extensions

two press-studs

selection of odd buttons for the belt

coloured cords for the bangles

Mini dress

Using variegated pink and purple yarn and 4mm (US 6) needles, cast on 70 sts.
rows 1–5: GS.
rows 6–24: SS for 19 rows, beginning and ending with a purl row.
row 25: K2tog, K15, K2tog, K10, K2tog, K8, K2tog, K10, K2tog, K15, K2tog [64 sts].
row 26: purl.
row 27: K2tog, K13, K2tog, K10, K2tog, K6, K2tog, K10, K2tog, K13, K2tog [58 sts].
rows 28–34: SS for 7 rows, beginning and ending with a purl row.
row 35: K2tog, K10, K2tog, K8, K2tog, K10, K2tog, K8, K2tog, K10, K2tog [52 sts].
rows 36–40: SS for 5 rows, beginning and ending with a purl row.

Armhole left back

row 41: K14, turn, and work on these sts only.
rows 42–51: SS for 10 rows.

Shoulder

row 52: P2tog twice, purl to end [12 sts].
row 53: knit.
rows 54–55: repeat rows 52 and 53 [10 sts].
Cast off purlwise.

Front

Rejoin the yarn.
row 56: K24, turn, and work on these sts only [24 sts].
row 57: purl.
row 58: K2tog, knit to last 2 sts, K2tog [22 sts].
rows 59–68: SS for 10 rows.

Shoulder

row 69: P2tog twice, purl to last 4 sts, P2tog twice [18 sts].
row 70: knit.
rows 71–72: repeat rows 69 and 70 [14 sts].
Cast off purlwise.

Armhole right back

Rejoin yarn.
row 73: knit [14 sts].
rows 74–83: SS for 10 rows.
row 84: purl to last 4 sts, P2tog twice [12 sts].
row 85: knit.
rows 86–87: repeat rows 84 and 85 [10 sts].
Cast off purlwise.

Making up

Fold the dress in half lengthways, right sides together. Mark a point 4cm (1½in) from the back neck opening. Sew from this point to the hem of the dress. Re-fold and pin the front and back shoulders together. Sew, neaten any loose ends and turn right-side out.

Button belt

Cut a 50cm (19¾in) length of black yarn. Thread one end through a needle that will pass through the holes in the buttons. Thread on each button through both holes so that they sit flat. Space them so they almost touch but don't bunch up. Tie off each end of the belt to secure.

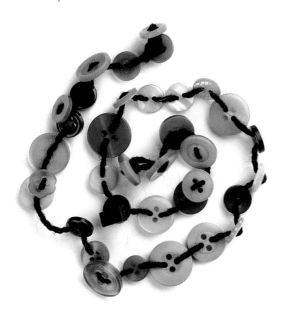

Choker necklace

Using 4mm (US 6) needles and black yarn, cast on 32 sts.
row 1: (K2, P2) to end of row.
row 2: (P2, K2) to end of row.
rows 3–4: repeat rows 1 and 2.
Cast off.
Neaten any loose threads. Sew a press-stud to the ends of the choker so that when it is done up the ends overlap.

tip

To make a smaller choker, reduce the number of cast-on stitches by a multiple of two. To make it into a belt, increase the number of cast-on stitches to 38. You can make a wider belt/choker by knitting more rows.

Waistcoat

Back

Using 4mm (US 6) needles and yellow-green yarn, cast on 54 sts.
rows 1–5: GS.
row 6: K4, purl to last 4 sts, K4.
row 7: knit.
rows 8–9: repeat rows 6 and 7.

Armhole left front

row 10: K14, turn, and work on these sts only.
row 11: purl to last 4 sts, K4.
row 12: knit.
rows 13–18: repeat rows 11 and 12.
row 19: purl to last 5 sts, K3, K2tog [13 sts].
row 20: knit.
row 21: P2tog twice, P4, K3, K2tog [10 sts].
row 22: knit.
row 23: P2tog twice, P1, knit to end [8 sts].
row 24: K2tog, knit to end [7 sts].
Cast off purlwise.

Back

Rejoin the yarn and work on the next 26 sts.
rows 25–34: SS for 10 rows [26 sts].

Shoulders

row 35: K2tog, knit to last 2 sts, K2tog [24 sts].
row 36: purl.
row 37: repeat row 35 [22 sts].
Cast off purlwise.

Armhole right front

Rejoin the yarn and work on the remaining 14 sts.
row 38: knit.
row 39: K4, purl to end of row.
row 40: knit.
rows 41–46: repeat rows 39 and 40.
row 47: K2tog, K4, purl to end [13 sts].
row 48: knit.
row 49: K2tog, K3, P4, P2tog twice [10 sts].
row 50: knit.
row 51: knit to last 5 sts, P1, P2tog twice [8 sts].
row 52: K to last 2 sts, K2tog.
Cast off purlwise.

Making up

Fold the waistcoat with right sides together and pin at the shoulders. Back stitch along each shoulder seam, neaten off the loose threads and tie off. Turn right-side out.

Underwear

Using 3mm (US 3) needles and blue yarn, cast on 24 sts.
rows 1–3: GS.
rows 4–6: SS, beginning and ending with a purl row.
row 7: K2tog, knit to last 2 sts, K2tog [22 sts].
row 8: P2tog, purl to last 2 sts, P2tog [20 sts].
rows 9–16: repeat rows 7 and 8 until 4 sts remain.
rows 17–20: SS for 4 rows, beginning with a knit row and ending with a purl row.
row 21: knit, inc in first and last st [6 sts].
row 22: purl, inc in first and last st [8 sts].
rows 23–30: repeat rows 21 and 22 until there are 24 sts on the needle.

rows 31–34: SS for 4 rows, beginning and ending with a knit row.
row 35: knit.
Cast off knitwise.

Making up

Fold the panties in half, right sides facing. Back stitch the small side seams. Neaten any loose ends and turn right-side out. If you wish, chain stitch a simple daisy design on to the pants in contrasting colours.

Beret

Using 10mm (US 15) needles and multicoloured fluffy yarn, cast on 40 sts.
rows 1–10: GS.
row 11: K2tog across the row [20 sts].
rows 12 and 13: repeat row 11 until 5 sts remain.
row 14: K2tog, K1, K2tog.
Cast off.
Fold the hat in half and sew down the seam.
Crochet a cord approximately 40cm (15¾in) long. Leave a loose end and thread it into a tapestry needle. Weave the cord in and out of the outer edge of the beret. Pull the cord to shape the beret. If you prefer, knit the cord following the instructions on page 25.

Rose

Rose adores swimming. Her long, thick hair tones perfectly with the muted russet, oranges and browns I have chosen for her outfit. Her swimsuit doubles as a halterneck top, which Rose wears with a matching mini skirt and a warm scarf. She also has a shoulder bag – useful for carrying her towel and other accessories to and from the pool.

Making the body

Follow the instructions on pages 58–61 for making the body using light brown yarn, and pages 12–14 for creating the face. Use a large pair of brown eyes and red lips, provided as templates on pages 78–79. Rose's eyebrows are cut from brown felt, using the templates provided, and I have tinted her eye area and cheeks using purple and pink acrylic paint (see page 14). For her hair, I have used masses of thick, dark brown yarn and attached it to her head using the rooted method (see page 15), together with a short fringe.

materials

Needles: 3mm (US 3), 4mm (US 6) and 10mm (US 15)

Crochet hook: 3mm (US 1 or C/D)

Yarns:

50g balls of yarn in light brown for the body, flecked russet-coloured yarn for the swimsuit, orange and yellow-brown for the skirt, multicoloured fluffy textured yarn for the scarf, yellow-brown and dark brown for the bag, and purple for the shoes

thick, dark brown yarn for the hair

Other materials:

half a pillow, or approx. 250g (9oz), of polyester fibrefill (you will probably use less)

old paintbrush for stuffing

either 3 empty toilet rolls or a piece of thick cardboard measuring 20 x 6cm (7¾ x 2¼in)

adhesive tape

tapestry needle

white felt for eyes, and red felt for mouth

acrylic paints in brown, black and white for painting the eyes, and purple and red for adding tints to the eye area and cheeks

gloss acrylic varnish for sealing the eyes and making them shine

glue suitable for sticking felt to wool, e.g. PVA or a clear craft glue

brown felt for eyebrows

press-stud

beads to decorate the tie for the skirt

Swimsuit

Using russet-coloured yarn and 4mm (US 6) needles, cast on 24 sts.

rows 1–3: knit.

rows 4–6: SS, beginning and ending with a purl row.

row 7: K2tog, knit to last 2 sts, K2tog [22 sts].

row 8: P2tog, purl to last 2 sts, P2tog [20 sts].

rows 9–16: repeat rows 7 and 8 until 4 sts remain.

rows 17–20: SS for 4 rows, beginning with a knit row and ending with a purl row.

row 21: knit, inc in first and last st [6 sts].

row 22: purl, inc in first and last st [8 sts].

rows 23–30: repeat rows 21 and 22 until 24 sts on needle, ending with a purl row.

rows 31–40: SS, ending with a purl row.

row 41: K2tog, knit to last 2 sts, K2tog [22 sts].

row 42: purl.

rows 43–55: repeat rows 41 and 42 until 8 sts remain.

rows 56–60: SS for 5 rows, beginning and ending with a purl row.

row 61: knit, inc in first and last st [10 sts].

row 62: purl.

rows 63–75: repeat rows 61 and 62 until 24 sts on needle, ending on a knit row.

rows 76–81: SS for 6 rows.

rows 82–84: GS.

row 85: K2tog twice, knit to last 4 sts, K2tog twice [20 sts].

row 86: K2tog, K6, K2tog twice, K6, K2tog [16 sts].

row 87: K2tog, K4, K2tog twice, K4, K2tog [12 sts].

Turn and work on first 6 sts only.

row 88: K2tog, K2, K2tog [4 sts].

Continue working in GS on these 4 sts until strap measures 6cm (2¼in).

next row: K2tog.

Cast off.

Repeat for other side.

Making up

1. Fold the piece with right sides together so the bottom parts match up. Pin and back stitch down the side seams of the lower part of the swimsuit. Neaten any loose threads and turn right-side out.

2. Make the strap going across the back of the swimsuit. On one side of the swimsuit, just below the garter stitch chest band, pick up 4 stitches on the needle and garter stitch a strap about 8.5cm (3in) long. Cast off and stitch this end to the other side of the swimsuit.

3. Sew a press-stud on to each end of the straps to create a halterneck.

Mini skirt

Using yellow-brown yarn and 4mm (US 6) needles, cast on 56 sts.

row 1: (K2, P2) to end of row.
row 2: (P2, K2) to end of row.
rows 3–4: repeat rows 1 and 2.
rows 5–7: SS, beginning and ending with a purl row.
rows 8–9: change to orange yarn and continue in SS for two rows.
row 10: (K1 yellow-brown, K2 orange) to end of row.
row 11: P1 orange, then (P1 yellow-brown, P2 orange) to end of row.
rows 12–15: SS in yellow-brown.
row 16: (K3 yellow-brown, K1 orange) to end of row.
row 17: (P1 orange, P3 yellow-brown) to end of row.
Return to yellow-brown only for remainder of knitting.
rows 18–20: SS, beginning with a knit row and ending with a purl row.
row 21: (K2, P2) to end of row.
row 22: (P2, K2) to end of row.
rows 23–24: repeat rows 21 and 22.
Cast off knitwise.

Making up

1. Fold the skirt in half, right sides together. Back stitch down the centre back seam.

2. Cut a length of yellow-brown yarn approximately 25cm (9¾in) long. Thread it into a tapestry needle and weave it in and out of the band of ribbing right around the waist.

3. Finish off the loose ends with beads and knot the ends to neaten. When the skirt is on the doll, draw in the tie to fit.

Scarf

Using 10mm (US 15) needles and fluffy textured yarn, cast on 12 sts.
GS until the desired length is reached. 30cm (11¾in) is a good scarf length, but you can make it shorter or longer if you wish.

Shoulder bag

Using yellow-brown and 4mm (US 6) needles, cast on 20 sts.

row 1: (K2, P2) to end of row.
row 2: (P2, K2) to end of row.
rows 3–4: repeat rows 1 and 2.
row 5: repeat row 1.
rows 6–9: SS, beginning and ending with a purl row.
Introduce the second colour in the next row.
row 10: (K2 yellow-brown, K2 dark brown) to end of row.
row 11: (P2 dark brown, P2 yellow-brown) to end of row.
rows 12–13: SS in yellow-brown.
rows 14–15: SS in dark brown.
rows 16–17: SS in yellow-brown.
row 18: (K2 yellow-brown, K2 dark brown) to end of row.
row 19: (P2 dark brown, P2 yellow-brown) to end of row.
rows 20–21: SS in yellow-brown.
rows 22–23: SS in dark brown.
rows 24–29: SS in yellow-brown.
rows 30–31: SS in dark brown.
rows 32–33: SS in yellow-brown.
row 34: (K2 yellow-brown, K2 dark brown) to end of row.
row 35: (P2 dark brown, P2 yellow-brown) to end of row.

rows 36–37: SS in yellow-brown.
rows 38–39: SS in dark brown.
rows 40–41: SS in yellow-brown.
rows 42–43: Repeat rows 34 and 35.
Continue in yellow-brown only.
rows 44–47: SS.
row 48: (K2, P2) to end of row.
row 49: (P2, K2) to end of row.
rows 50–51: repeat rows 48 and 49.
Cast off in pattern.

Making up

1. Fold the piece in half, right sides together. Back stitch down the two side seams. Turn right-side out.

2. To make the strap, crochet three strands of yarn together, two in yellow-brown and one in dark brown. Make the strap approximately 35cm (13¾in) long. Stitch the strap up one side of the bag starting at the bottom corner, then take it down the other side. If you prefer, make the strap by plaiting the three strands of yarn together.

3. Create the fringe along the bottom of the bag by hooking through short lengths of yarn using a crochet hook and tying them in a knot.

Shoes

Make two.

Using 3mm (US 3) needles and purple yarn, cast on 3 sts.
row 1: knit, inc in each st [6 sts].
row 2: purl.
row 3: knit, inc in each st [12 sts].
row 4: purl.
row 5: knit, inc 1 st at each end [14 sts].
row 6: purl.
row 7: knit, inc 1 st at each end [16 sts].
rows 8–10: SS.
row 11: K5, cast off 6 sts, K5.
Turn shoe and work on these
5 sts only.
rows 12–16: SS for 5 rows,
beginning and ending with a purl
row. Do not cast off. Cut yarn
(leaving a long tail) and either
leave sts on needle or transfer
them to a stitch holder.
Return to other set of 5 sts and
work as follows:
rows 17–20: SS for 4 rows.
row 21: cast on 6 sts and purl to end.
row 22: K11 then continue on the
remaining 5 sts. (If sts transferred to
stitch holder then transfer them back
to needle.) You will now have a
knitted row of 16 sts.
row 23: purl [16 sts].
row 24: Cast off knitwise.

Making up

Weave all loose strands into the knitting and trim,
tightening any holes created by loose stitches as you work.
Fold the shoe in half, right sides together, and back stitch
up the back seam. Turn and the shoe is finished.

Chloe

This stylish beach babe just cannot get enough of the sun! I have dressed her in a bright red bikini and matching choker necklace to show off her fiery personality, and her long, multicoloured hair reflects her sunny dispostion. For cooler days she wears a bright blue and green wrap tied around her waist – a whole rainbow of colours for this colourful girl!

Making the body

Make the body following the instructions on pages 58–61 using brown yarn, and red and black yarn for the stripy legs. Create the face following the notes given on pages 12–14, using a large pair of brown eyes and pink lips provided as templates on pages 78–79. Chloe's eyebrows are cut from black felt, also using the templates provided. For her hair, I have used a textured, multicoloured novelty yarn and attached it to her head using the rooted method (see page 15).

materials

Needles: 3mm (US 3), 4mm (US 6) and 10mm (US 15)

Crochet hook: 3mm (US 1 or C/D)

Yarns:

50g balls of yarn in brown for the body, red and black for the legs, bikini and choker necklace, multicoloured eyelash or other fluffy novelty yarn in shades of blue, green and purple for the wrap, and thick, textured multicoloured yarn for the hair

Other materials:

half a pillow, or approx. 250g (9oz), of polyester fibrefill (you will probably use less)

old paintbrush for stuffing

either 3 empty toilet rolls or a piece of thick cardboard measuring 20 x 6cm (7¾ x 2¼in)

adhesive tape

tapestry needle

white felt for eyes, and pink felt for mouth

acrylic paints in brown, black and white for painting the eyes

gloss acrylic varnish for sealing the eyes and making them shine

glue suitable for sticking felt to wool, e.g. PVA or a clear craft glue

black felt for eyebrows

four black beads to decorate the ties on the bikini top

hook and eye

Wrap

Using 10mm (US 15) needles and multicoloured eyelash
(or other fluffy) yarn, cast on 5 sts.
Working in GS:
row 1: knit, inc 1 st at beginning and end of row.
Repeat row 1 until the wrap is approximately 60cm
(23½in) wide along the longest edge.
Cast off.

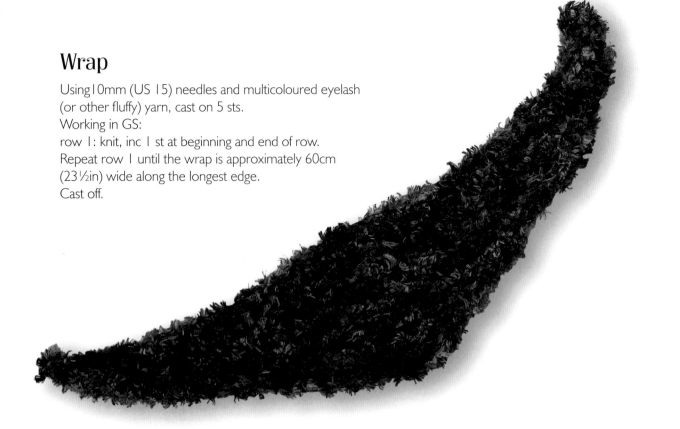

Bikini

Bottom

Using red yarn and 3mm (US 3) needles, cast on 24 sts.
rows 1–3: GS.
rows 4–6: SS, beginning and ending with a purl row.
row 7: K2tog, knit to last 2 sts, K2tog [22 sts].
row 8: P2tog, purl to last 2 sts, P2tog [20 sts].
rows 9–16: repeat rows 7 and 8 until 4 sts remain.
rows 17–20: SS, beginning with a knit row and ending
with a purl row.
row 21: knit, inc in first and last st [6 sts].
row 22: purl, inc in first and last st [8 sts].
rows 23–30: repeat rows 21 and 22 until 24 sts
on needle.
rows 31–34: SS, beginning with a knit row.
row 35: knit.
Cast off knitwise.

Making up

Fold the piece in half, right sides facing. Back stitch the
small side seams and neaten any loose ends. Turn right-
side out.
If you wish, chain stitch a simple daisy in
contrasting colours.

Top

Cast on 34 sts.

rows 1–4: GS.

row 5: K2tog, knit to last 2 sts, K2tog [32 sts].

row 6: P2tog, purl to last 2 sts, P2tog [30 sts].

rows 7–8: repeat rows 5 and 6 until 26 sts remain.

row 9: K2tog, K9, K2tog twice, K9, K2tog [22 sts].

row 10: P2tog, P8, P2tog, P8, P2tog [19 sts].

row 11: K2tog, K7, K2tog, K6, K2tog [16 sts].

Turn and work back over the first 8 sts only.

row 12: P2tog, P4, P2tog.

Turn and work on these 6 sts only.

row 13: K2tog, K2, K2tog [4 sts].

row 14: P2tog twice.

Cast off.

Rejoin yarn and work the last 3 rows on the other side.

Making up

1. Neaten off any loose ends. Fold the top in half and back stitch along the short centre back seam. Turn right-side out.

2. Crochet two ties for the halterneck top, each approximately 10cm (4in) long. Decorate with black beads and tie the ends in a knot to secure. Alternatively, the ties can be knitted (see page 25).

Choker necklace

Crochet three cords – one black and two red – each 24cm (9½in) long. Leave a tail of yarn approximately 7cm (2¾in) long at each end. Tie the cords together at each end of the crocheted section and attach a hook to one knot and the corresponding eye to the other. Use this to secure the choker when it is wrapped around the doll's neck.

If you prefer, the necklace can be knitted. Simply cast on 1 stitch and knit until the cord is of the desired length.

Templates

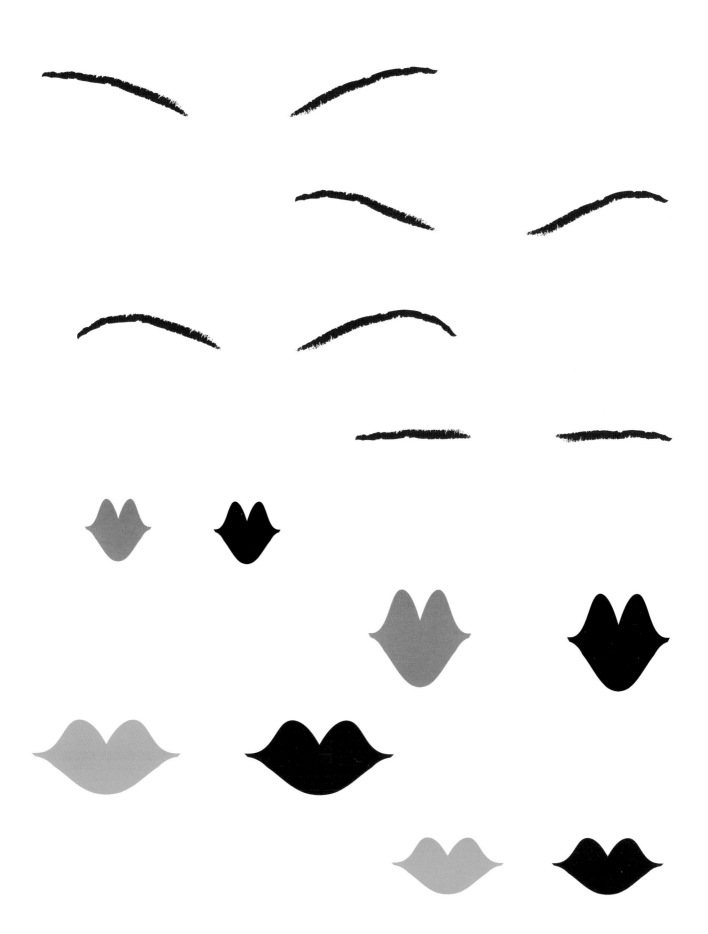

Index